Scholastic's The Magic School Bus®

PLAYS BALL
A Book About Forces

SCHOLASTIC INC.
New York Toronto London Auckland Sydney

From an episode of the animated TV series
produced by Scholastic Productions, Inc.
Based on *The Magic School Bus* books
written by Joanna Cole and illustrated by Bruce Degen.

TV tie-in adaptation by Nancy E. Krulik and illustrated by Art Ruiz.
TV script written by John May, Brian Meehl, and Jocelyn Stevenson.

ISBN 0-590-92240-8

12 11 10 9   1 2/0

Printed in the U.S.A.   24

First Scholastic printing, August 1997

When most classes play baseball, they go out on the field. But that's not what happens when you have a teacher like Ms. Frizzle.

In our class, when we play baseball, we go on a field *trip*!

It all started during recess. We were playing baseball. Ralphie was at bat, Wanda was pitching. The rest of us had taken our positions in the field. There was only one thing missing.

"Hey, Wanda, where's home plate?" Ralphie asked.

"There isn't one," Wanda replied. "You'll have to pretend."

But I'll have nothing to slide into when I hit a home run!

Wanda began her pitch. She lifted her leg high, reached back and . . .

Suddenly, Dorothy Ann raced out onto the field. "Hey, you guys!" she shouted. "Check this out. I just found the coolest thing!"

Ralphie scowled. "*Dorothy Ann!*" he said with a groan. "Not now. I'm one swing away from hitting my way into the record books."

"But you've got to see this. It will change your lives," Dorothy Ann insisted. She held up a book. It was called *A Child's Garden of Physics*.

Everyone burst out laughing. Change our lives? We didn't think so!

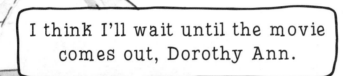

I think I'll wait until the movie comes out, Dorothy Ann.

"I'm really happy for you, Dorothy Ann," Ralphie said. "But right now, I've got a game-winning homer to hit!"

"But you don't understand," Dorothy Ann said. "This book is all about what gets things moving, and what makes them stop. Forces! Friction! Pushes! Pulls!"

Nothing could stop Dorothy Ann when she was on a roll! "Okay, picture a big, red sled sitting in the snow," she explained. "It's not going anywhere. But if somebody comes along and gives the sled a push, it will move. That's a force.

"The sled will keep moving until something stops it — like some dirt," she continued. "Things rubbing together cause a force called friction. And the sled stops because the dirt is pushing it against the direction it's moving. This force against the runners is the friction in action. Friction slows down and stops nearly every motion on Earth."

Okay, so now we knew what friction was. But what we didn't know was why Dorothy Ann thought it was so important.

Ralphie was tired of hearing about friction. He picked up his bat and tapped at the dirt where home plate should have been. Then he remembered Dorothy Ann's book. *The book would make a great home plate*, Ralphie thought. It was flat, white, and just the right size.

"Hey, Dorothy Ann, that book does sound kind of cool," he said.

"It is, Ralphie," Dorothy Ann agreed happily. She thought Ralphie wanted to *read* the book. "And look at this. Right here on page ninety-seven."

Ralphie looked at the page. It showed a picture of a baseball field.

"It would be impossible to play baseball on that field," Dorothy Ann told Ralphie. "There's no friction there."

Ralphie grinned. Now he had a home plate. "Let's play ball!" he called out.

But before we could get back on the field, we heard a familiar honking coming from the parking lot. It was the Magic School Bus!

"All aboard!" Ms. Frizzle cried out from the driver's seat.

We all ran to the bus. Ralphie dropped Dorothy Ann's book as he raced over.

"Today we're going to a baseball game," Ms. Frizzle announced.

We were confused. A baseball game wasn't new, or different, or exciting, like most of our field trips were.

"Ms. Frizzle, can we go someplace really unusual?" Dorothy Ann asked. She turned to Ralphie. "Like that place I showed you, Ralphie. You know, page ninety-seven. Show them."

Ralphie stared out the window as we passed the baseball field. Dorothy Ann followed his glance. She gasped. Her book was lying in the dirt.

"Ralphie! How could you?" Dorothy Ann asked.

"Don't worry, Dorothy Ann," Ms. Frizzle assured her. "We'll get your book and keep Ralphie happy, too! Bus! Do your stuff!" she shouted.

The Magic School Bus barreled across the playground in the direction of Dorothy Ann's book. The bus spun around and around. Dorothy Ann's book blew open, and . . . we drove right into it!

We watched through the windows as the pages flipped by.

"Ms. Frizzle! Stop here!" Dorothy Ann shouted excitedly. "It's page ninety-seven! The page I was talking about! It's all about a World Without Friction!"

"It looks like the World of Baseball to me!" Ralphie said.

The bus ground to a halt. Ralphie raced out the door. "Come on!" he said.

"Ralphie, watch out," Dorothy Ann warned. "The ground on that field has no friction!"

Without anything to push against, like the friction of his feet against the ground, Ralphie couldn't stop. He bounced off one wall, slid across the field, and crashed into another wall.

We lowered ourselves onto the baseball field. We slipped and slid across the field. It felt like ice skating (only without the skates).

Ms. Frizzle blew her whistle. It was time for the game to begin. But without any friction to help us stop, we couldn't get into our positions. What were we going to do?

Just then, the bus flew overhead. It had turned into a Magic School Bus-Blimp. Liz was in the driver's seat. She pushed a button and a giant crane dropped down from the bus. The crane lifted us up like bowling pins and placed us in our positions on the field.

"Play ball!" Ms. Frizzle cried out.

"Welcome to the All-Frizzle Friction-Free Baseball Classic," Ms. Frizzle announced into her microphone. "The ground out there has no friction, we repeat, *no* friction!"

"Well, folks, believe it or not, we're coming to you from inside my textbook," Dorothy Ann added. "Our playing field is slipperier than ice!"

Wanda got ready to throw her first pitch. She lifted her leg, pulled back her arm, and hurled the ball at Ralphie. The ball raced in Ralphie's direction. But Wanda slid backward toward second base!

"And look at that, folks," Dorothy Ann announced. "The force Wanda used really got that ball going and pushed her way back toward second base!"

Ralphie kept his eye on the ball. He swung as it sailed over the plate. *Crack!* Ralphie hit a hot grounder right down the third base line. Carlos tried to scoop up the ball. But without any friction to slow it down, the ball was going too fast to catch — it sped right past him.

We waited for Ralphie to run to first base. But he didn't run. The force of the swinging bat started Ralphie spinning in circles. Ralphie *spun* his way to first. And he kept on spinning around the bases.

Just as he was about to reach home, Ralphie slammed right into Dorothy Ann! They grabbed on to each other and spun around the field.

"Ms. Frizzle," Dorothy Ann suggested, "I think we'd better call this game — due to lack of friction."

Ms. Frizzle agreed. "Game!" she called out.

It was time to get back on the bus and go back to the world *with* friction.

Liz pulled out a pin from inside the bus and popped the blimp like a balloon. The bus whizzed on and finally landed safely just outside the frictionless baseball field.

Now, all we had to do was get on the bus. But without friction to help us walk, how could we reach the bus?

Suddenly, the hood ornament on the front of the bus shot out, trailing a rope behind it. The ornament hooked itself onto a wall across the field. "Grab on, class," Ms. Frizzle ordered. We reached up and took the rope in our hands.

"A push is one force that can get us moving," Ms. Frizzle said. "What's the opposite?"

Wanda gripped the rope tightly. "A pull?" she grunted.

Ms. Frizzle smiled. "Excellent!" she said.

And so we *pulled* ourselves, hand over hand, down the rope, and off the frictionless field.

I knew I should have stayed home today!

We'd never realized that friction did so much. We all owed Dorothy Ann a big apology for laughing at her.

"Wow!" Wanda exclaimed. "You were right, Dorothy Ann."

"Can I borrow your book when Ralphie's through with it?" Tim asked.

"Me too?" Arnold said.

"Then me?" Carlos chimed in.

"Wait a sec," Ralphie interrupted. "No one gets the book — until we get out of it!"

In my old school we pressed *flowers* in our books.

We piled into the bus, sat down, and buckled up our seat belts. It was getting a little windy outside, so we shut the windows tight.

"Let's book it!" Ms. Frizzle said. She put the key in the ignition. But before the bus could move we heard a loud, scary *BOOM*!

The wind had lifted the cover of Dorothy Ann's book right off the ground. The cover (and about 50 pages) had smacked down onto the bus!

We had to get out of there . . . and fast!

"Any suggestions, class?" Ms. Frizzle asked us.

"Better floor it, Ms. Frizzle," Wanda proposed.

Ms. Frizzle pushed down on the gas pedal. The engine roared. The wheels spun. But the bus didn't budge.

"Oh no!" Dorothy Ann exclaimed. "The cover of the book is pushing down so hard that it's creating too much friction for the wheels to push us out!"

We're stu-uh-uh-uck!

I guess we'll be food for the BOOKworms!

"I can't believe this!" Ralphie said. "We're stuck in Dorothy Ann's book."

"What will happen to us if we can't get out?" Phoebe asked nervously.

Ms. Frizzle just smiled. "As I always say, those who are book bound should take a look around." She opened the bus door and leaped outside. "This way, class."

We really, really didn't want to get out of the bus. But we didn't want to be stuck inside the book without our teacher, either. So we followed Ms. Frizzle onto page ninety-seven of Dorothy Ann's book.

Keesha tried to gather all the facts. "Okay, where do we stand?" she asked.

"Uh, somewhere between pages ninety-six and ninety-seven," Carlos teased.

Keesha frowned. That was *not* what she meant! "Carlos!" Keesha scolded.

"Hey, I was just trying to lighten things up," he apologized.

Tim smiled. Carlos had just given him a great idea!

"Lighten things up!" Tim exclaimed. "That's it! We'll climb up on the roof and *push* up on the book."

Keesha looked at him. "You're saying we should hold up the book, get in the bus, and drive away . . . "

Tim nodded.

"How?" Arnold asked him.

"Good question, Arnold," Ms. Frizzle remarked. "Anyone have an answer?"

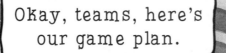

Okay, teams, here's our game plan.

Dorothy Ann had another idea. "Look, the letters peel off the page," she said as she stripped off a lowercase *t*. "I have a plan! We'll split into two teams. Ralphie's team goes on the roof of the bus and pushes up on the book. At the same time, my team piles letters near the book's spine. That will hold the book open long enough for us to get back in the bus and drive away."

"Excellent plan," Ralphie told Dorothy Ann. "But why doesn't *your* team push up on the book while *my* team piles the letters? Okay?"

Dorothy Ann stared angrily at Ralphie. "Not okay!" she replied.

"Yes, okay!" Ralphie insisted.

"Not!" Dorothy Ann declared.

Arnold walked up and interrupted their argument. "Um, Dorothy Ann, what is it again that makes everything stop?" he asked.

Dorothy Ann looked confused. Why was Arnold asking her this now? "Friction," she replied, curiously.

Arnold turned to Ralphie. "If there's a lot of friction, you can't get anywhere, right, Ralphie?" he asked.

Ralphie nodded.

"Well, I think there's a little too much friction between you two," Arnold said. "So if we're ever going to get out of this book . . . "

"We're going to have to get rid of the friction between us," Dorothy Ann and Ralphie said together.

They reached out and shook hands.

It's a good thing I didn't stay home today.

It took a little while, but we finally piled enough letters in the spine of the book to hold the cover open. Ms. Frizzle led us back on the bus, and we zoomed right out of Dorothy Ann's book.

As soon as the bus stopped on the school baseball field, Ralphie raced for the door.

"Wait a minute, Ralphie," Dorothy Ann warned. "Remember what happened the last time you jumped out of the bus like that?"

Ralphie nodded. Dorothy Ann stepped in front of him. She slowly stepped down to the ground. She moved her foot back and forth in the sand.

"Never fear! There's friction here!" she assured Ralphie.

We couldn't wait to play a game of friction-filled baseball. Dorothy Ann was the first one at bat. Wanda pitched the ball, Dorothy Ann swung, and . . . *craaack*. Dorothy Ann exerted a lot of force on that ball.

Carlos was out in left field. Would he be able to apply *his* force and stop the ball? Carlos held his glove high in the air, but the ball soared right over his head. Finally, the ball dropped to the ground and rolled. Luckily for Carlos, friction caused by the grass pushing against the forward motion of the ball slowed the ball to a stop.

Carlos scooped up the ball and threw it across the field. Dorothy Ann slid for home. *But where was home plate?*

It took us a while, but we finally found home plate. Ralphie was *reading* it! "Dorothy Ann was right," he said. "This book is great!"

Letters to the Editor

Dear Editor,
I would really like to find a copy of Dorothy Ann's textbook, but I went to my library, and there's nothing like it in the non-friction section. Does this mean that here on Earth, friction is the only game in town?
Forcefully yours,
A Frizzle Fan

Dear Fan,
You're right. Friction is the only game in town. But there are ways of giving friction the slip. You do that every time you go down a slide or go skateboarding, waterskiing, or snow skiing. Friction is all around us. But sometimes there's less of it.
—The Editor

Dear Editor,
I go to Phoebe's old school. We never go on field trips like the ones Ms. Frizzle takes her class on. I don't mean to be pushy, but how far do I need to go to experience forces?
Sincerely,
Phoebe's Friend

Dear Friend,
Forces are simply pushes and pulls. And those exist just about everywhere you are — so look no farther than your home, or school, or, of course, your local baseball field!
—The Editor

From the Desk of Ms. Frizzle

A note to parents, teachers, and kids

Take chances! Ask questions! Go on a field trip — in your own backyard! Here are two ways you can experiment with forces and motion.

1. TUG-OF-WAR

Forces are pushes and pulls. All pushes and pulls have strength, like how hard we push and how hard we are pulled. When two evenly matched teams play tug-of-war and neither team wins, the two pulls have canceled each other out. But if you add a new teammate to one side, it's sure to put more pull in that direction!

2. KICKBALL

If you have a ball, you can experiment with friction. We know that friction works by pushing against the direction that something is moving. But different surfaces apply different amounts of friction. Which surface applies more friction — sand, grass, cement, or polished wood? To find out, give your ball a little force to get it rolling (a kick or a push will do) across each of those different surfaces. You'll find that the more slippery the surface, the less friction.

Ms. Frizzle